out door gym - pg 104

BEIJING AT
Play

Common People's Approach to Health and Happiness

Two Sisters' Journey into the Park-Culture of Beijing

Hongmei Lu & Dongmei Lu

China Intercontinental Press

本书是以新闻采访、新闻纪录的形式，展现北京独特的公园文化，旨在向世界介绍北京百姓如何娱乐健身、享受生活、延年益寿。

图书在版编目（CIP）数据

玩在北京：英文/路红梅 路冬梅著.
—北京：五洲传播出版社，2008.5
ISBN 978-7-5085-1290-7
Ⅰ.玩… Ⅱ.①路…②路… Ⅲ.①中年人—体育锻炼—概括—北京市—英文
②老年人—体育锻炼—概括—北京市—英文 Ⅳ.G812-71
中国版本图书馆CIP数据核字（2008）第058093号

选题编辑：荆孝敏
责任编辑：张美景
装帧设计：刘 鹏

玩在北京

五洲传播出版社
地址：北京市海淀区北小马厂6号华天大厦24层
邮编：100038
电话：(86-10) 58891280/58880274
网址：www.cicc.org.cn/books

印刷：北京画中画印刷有限公司
开本：1/16
印张：15
版次：2008年6月第1版第1次印刷
印量：1-2000
书号：ISBN 978-7-5085-1290-7
定价：109.00元

We do not know a nation until we know its pleasures of life, just as we do not know a man until we know how he spends his leisure.

—Lin Yutang, *My Country and My People*

To the Joyful People of Beijing.

献给热爱生活的人们。

INTRODUCTION

玩

Not until you walk into a local park in Beijing, do you realize that the Chinese style of fitness goes far beyond Taiji (Tai Chi) practice – there are games like a big Yo-Yo played with a pair of sticks, a giant colorful feather "Hacky Sac" kicked in the air by a circle of people, and singing and dancing openly enjoyed by hundreds.

Join us as we explore together the park culture of Beijing. We will show you that Taiji can be performed with a pair of colorful fans; calligraphy can be practiced with water on paved ground; walking in a four-step fashion to the beat of drums can be quite exhilarating; and harmonica playing can lure hundreds of people to sing and dance along.

"Come and play with us!" you just might get invited by a Kongzhu group or by a gentleman who wants to show you a few waltz steps. You may hear some "playful" greetings among the locals:

"Where did you go to play this morning?"
"Have you played today?"
"Played any new games lately?"
"After we eat, we play."

Play, to the residents of Beijing, means to exercise without stress and competition, to savor their childhood, and to explore new interests into even very advanced age.

This is the park culture of Beijingers, people passionate about getting out and playing in parks or open spaces day or night. These self-promoted pleasures cost people almost nothing but bring them healthier and happier lives.

As your guides on this fascinating journey, we hope the experience doesn't stop at the exits of Beijing parks, but opens up a playful door to your own gratifying journey to health and happiness.

Dongmei Lu & Hongmei Lu

Self-Directed Play

There is no pressure, for *play* is self-driven;
There is no competition, for *play* is self-entertaining;
There is no judgment, for *play* is self-satisfying;
There is no restriction, for *play* is self-liberating.

Play creates joy;
Play stimulates the brain and strengthens the body;
Play connects people with common interests;
Play dissipates fear, loneliness and isolation.

The intention is to play;
The process is fun;
The result is a healthy workout.

Every morning, countless awakened enthusiasts gather in the parks where for hundreds of years the emperors of China had once indulged themselves in playful behavior. Now these backyard retreats of the imperial city have become the sanctuary of common people.

Today's *play* reigns yesterday's imperial gardens.

CONTENTS

Ancient Wisdom

A sage prevents disease instead of treating disease and prevents chaos instead of suppressing chaos. To cure an illness after it has occurred, or to calm a disturbance after it has broken out is like digging a well when one already feels thirsty, or forging weapons after the war has taken place. Would these actions not be too late?

—The *Yellow Emperor's Classic of Internal Medicine (Huangdi Neijing)*

　　是故圣人不治已病治未病，不治已乱治未乱，此之谓也。夫病已成而后药之，乱已成而后治之，譬犹渴而穿井，斗而铸锥，不亦晚乎。

Today's Collective Wisdom

(To engage oneself in preventive activities in order to promote one's health means:)

No personal suffering,
No burden on the family,
Minimize medical cost,
Benefit the general welfare of society.

—A popular refrain among common folk in China

个人不受罪　家人不受累
节省医药费　有利全社会

Taiji

Taiji means "Supreme Ultimate". The concept of "Supreme Ultimate" originally pointed to the universe in a cosmological sense and then it evolved into the foundation of Chinese philosophy, religion, literature, art, and medicine. Now when people talk about Taiji, it is automatically understood as the traditional Chinese martial art - Taiji Quan or known to the West as Tai Chi.

Taiji, the Supreme Ultimate, is depicted in the Taijitu or Yin-Yang symbol, a visual expression of the Supreme Ultimate Balance which creates the Great Harmony in everything in the universe.

Taiji philosophy draws its nourishment from Chinese ancient books such as *I Ching (The Book of Changes), Huangdi Neijing (The Yellow Emperor's Classic of Internal Medicine),* and *Dao De Jing (Tao Te Ching)*. According to Taiji philosophy, there are two opposing, yet interrelated forces: Yin and Yang, each of which includes elements of the other. Existing in all things in nature, these two forces are in constant stage of changing and balancing; one may transform into its opposite under certain conditions. Ultimately, the balanced interaction between Yin and Yang will create a Supreme situation, a harmonious whole as represented in the Yin-Yang circle.

This ancient philosophy of balancing opposite elements to create and maintain the Great Harmony has nourished and fostered the thought of many generations in China to raise the awareness of balance in every aspect of life, ranging from individual health, family and social life to an individual connection to nature. Every being is a small circle within the infinite big circle - the universe which is the ultimate whole or the unity of Oneness.

Traditional Chinese medicine (TCM) is rooted in Taiji philosophy and it states that ill health is a result of imbalance between Yin and Yang in one's body or mind; therefore, a well-balanced mind, body and spirit are essential to one's total well-being.

Applying Taiji philosophy, Chinese ancestors created Taiji Quan (Tai Chi) in an attempt to foster good health through a sequence of physical movements that guides and reminds us to create and maintain the Ultimate Yin-Yang balance for life. Hence Taiji Quan is Taiji philosophy in practice and it is a way of life. Similarly, other forms of Taiji such as Taiji sword, Taiji fan, and Taiji-Soft ball were created and developed based on the same principles and have been enjoyed by many practitioners.

1.1 Taiji Quan

1.2 Taiji Sword

1.3 Taiji Fan

1.4 Taiji Soft Ball

(See Chapter 5)

1.1 Taiji Quan

About Taiji Quan

DESCRIPTION:

Taiji Quan or Taiji, known to the West as Tai Chi, means *"Supreme Ultimate Fist"*, an internal Chinese martial art, created for promoting health and longevity. It applies Taiji philosophy or Yin-Yang theory into a sequence of fluid, gentle, and circular movements which allows practitioners to quiet their minds in order to explore their bodies and ultimately to achieve the unity and balance of the body, mind and spirit.

A BRIEF HISTORY:

The exact origin is vague from the existing record. The earliest version of Taiji Quan, however, was created from observation and imitation of nature: the stillness of mountains, the fluidity of rivers and the agile movements of animals. One example of this is an exercise called "Five Animals Play" created by a great Chinese physician Hua Tuo (147-208). This routine along with other similar routines are considered the embryonic forms of Taiji Quan.

The legendary Zhang San-feng. Legend says that a fun-loving Daoist (Taoist) Immortal, Zhang San-feng of the Song Dynasty (960-1279) created Taiji Quan after he had witnessed a fight between a sparrow and a snake. Also, Daoist monks have been credited for developing Taiji Quan as a method of self-cultivation of Daoism.

The five best known family styles. There are many styles of Taiji Quan created many centuries ago in different regions of China. The five best known styles started from Chen, then followed by Yang, Wu (two versions), and Sun, each named after the family that started the style.

The 24-Step Taiji Quan. Today most people in parks or elsewhere throughout the world practice a simplified version of Taiji Quan called the 24-Step Beijing Form compiled based on the Yang-style by the Chinese Sports Commission in 1956 with the goal of standardizing and popularizing Taiji Quan.

BENEFITS:

Along with Qigong, Taiji Quan is considered by traditional Chinese medicine a natural therapy that boosts practitioner's immune system by balancing Yin-Yang and promoting the free flow of Qi (or Chi, life energy).

China's earliest extant painting of medical gymnastics guide called "Daoyin," created at the end of 3rd century B.C.

The ancient version of Taiji-like practice can be traced back to the Spring and Autumn Period (770-476 B.C.) when people developed a sequence of gymnastics movements that combined dancing, stretching and breathing techniques to promote the circulation of Qi for fortifying the joints, alleviating aches and pains as well as improving physical conditions (see the unearthed picture - "Daoyin" on the left).

"Five Animals Play" was created by a great Chinese physician Hua Tuo (145-208), who adapted "Daoyin" routines into five groups of movements by mimicking tiger, deer, bear, monkey and bird.

"Five Animals Play"

"Bears" in *Changpuhe Park*

Led by Yang Chengfu, the grandson of the Yang-style founder, the modern form of Taiji Quan was established around the beginning of the 20th century.

The Yang-style Taiji Quan was later used as the platform of the simplified Taiji Quan called "24-Step Taiji Quan". Today it becomes a popular form around the world.

Taiji Quan master Yang Chengfu (1883-1936). In the Yang style, a posture called "Single Whip"

The same posture "Single Whip" is practiced today in the Yang-style 24-Step Taiji Quan sequence.

Step-10, wave hands as clouds: Circle arms while stepping sideways to the left.

Step-13, kick with right heel: Circle arms, open arms from the top and kick with right heel.

24-Step Taiji Quan

Each step has a poetic name (these names are not exclusive to one particular style of Taiji Quan). When practicing, people usually follow the 24-Step music tape which calls for each step with tranquil-background music to guide the practice.

Since this form is considered the most elementary and fundamental, it is enjoyed by many beginners and it usually takes about five minutes to perform.

Step-17, push down and stand on right leg: Drop on right leg, then lift left arm and left knee up.

Step-18, work at shuttles on both sides: Hold ball, then block and push.

Books on Taiji Quan (Tai Chi)

Master Liang, Shou-Yu & Wu, Wen-Ching. *Tai Chi Chuan: 24 & 48 Postures with Martial Applications*. Roslindale, MA: YMAA Publication Center, 1996.

Jahnke, Roger. *The Healing Promise of Qi: Creating Extraordinary Wellness Through Qigong and Tai Chi*. New York: Contemporary Book, 2002.

Kuo, Simmone. *Long Life Good Health trough Tai-Chi Chuan*. Berkeley, CA: North Atlantic Books, 1991.

24-Step Taiji Quan in *Changpuhe Park*

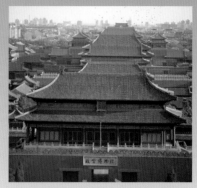

The north gate of the *Forbidden City*

Mr. Cao, a 86-year old traveler from Shaanxi Province is doing some self-formed Taiji Quan (a simple sequence of movements he practices every day at home) while waiting for the *gate of the Forbidden City* to open in the morning for touring.

Shichahai Lake

Chen-Style Taiji Quan

Originated around 1600s, Chen-style Taiji Quan is considered the forefather of the five main family-style Taiji Quan. Many Taiji practitioners like to advance themselves to Chen-style after they are comfortable with the 24-Step Taiji Quan.

1.2 Taiji Sword

太
极
劍

A park-goer's bicycle (The black case is a boom box that plays Taiji music.)

About Taiji Sword

It is an extension of Taiji Quan. It adheres to the principles of Taiji and integrates Taiji Quan and weapon into another meditative martial-and-healing art.

By the lotus lake, a little practitioner in *purple Bamboo Park*

The regulars in *Yuandadu Park*

Reflection of a Healthier and Happier Life

Ms. Tang, in her 60s, comes to the *Linglong Park* every morning practicing Taiji. "I retired early in my 40s due to my poor health. I felt so bad physically and mentally that I lost interest in living. But after I started learning Taiji, my health has been improving and I feel so much better now. I am a member of the Taiji-Folk Team of Beijing. Our team was invited to Japan not long ago for a culture-exchange program."

Ms. Tang's effort and passion for Taiji pay off. An impressive split in front of the *Linglong Pagoda*

1.3 Taiji Fan

太极扇

About Taiji Fan

Taiji Fan is another Taiji related martial art. It combines Taiji Quan (internal martial art), Gongfu (Kung Fu, external martial art) and dance movements to create a unique style of fitness program, both martial and elegant.

Morning sunshine illuminates the
regular Taiji-fan practitioners.

"Laying like a bow, standing like a pine tree, and sitting like a table clock…" a popular song used for Taiji-fan practice comes from a portable tape player. *Beihai Park*

"卧似一张弓，站似一棵松，不动不摇坐如钟，走路一阵风。
南拳和北腿，少林武当功，太极八卦连环掌，中华有神功"

Folk Games From Antiquity

Kongzhu (diabolo), Jianzi (Hacky Sac) and Fengzheng (kite) were invented about the same period in history, dated around the Han Dynasty (206 B.C.-220 A.D.). For more than 2,000 years, they have evolved yet stayed vigorous and timeless.

1.1 Kongzhu Playing

1.2 Shuttlecock Kicking (Hacky Sac)

1.3 Kite Flying

2.1 Kongzhu Playing

抖空竹

Kongzhus for Sale on a Tricycle

About Kongzhu

DESCRIPTION:

Kongzhu means hollow bamboo. Traditionally it is made of bamboo and/ or wood. Nowadays various materials are used, such as plastic, rubber and fiberglass. It is a big Yo-Yo spinning and whistling. See the photos below for different shapes. The size ranges from as small as half the size of an adult's palm to half the size of an adult's body.

HISTORY:

Originated in China about 2,000 years ago, matured during the Song Dynasty (960-1279), Kongzhu became a common folk-game during the Ming Dynasty (1368-1644) and the Qing Dynasty (1616-1911). Today Kongzhu still attracts hundreds of people in Beijing and other parts of China.

TECHNIQUES:

There are more than one-hundred documented techniques or tricks with Kongzhu playing. And there are infinite variations from players who are creative and ingenious. Often Kongzhu playing can be seen in a festival or an acrobatic performance in China due to its artful-entertainment value.

BENEFITS:

Playing Kongzhu provides a good practice for hand-eye coordination; over time it improves the player's agility, balance and flexibility. It is a game that is physical, stimulating, and therapeutic. Foremost, its entertainment value whether for self or for others is what makes it a timeless game.

Multi-layered and double-wheeled   Double-wheeled   Single-wheeled   Odd-shaped   Double-axle

It only takes five minutes to learn

About 8:30 a.m. by the beautiful lotus lake in *Purple Bamboo Park*, a lady appears in front of my camera and turns my attention from a dance group to her engrossing Kongzhu acting, brisk and artful.

Ms. Wang, 58, a Kongzhu master, teaches Kongzhu here every morning. "In five minutes, you can learn it," she tells everyone who shows interest in her eye-catching tactics. I couldn't resist the opportunity of learning Kongzhu (since I did get to learn it when I was a kid), so I put my camera in the backpack and became a student of hers.

Ms. Wang shows a trick called "fairy crossing the bridge."

The Kongzhu costs 30 Yuan (about $4) and the tuition is complimentary. Rocking the Kongzhu and making it spin on the string, I am thrilled to realize that it is easier than I thought. Indeed, in five minutes I get the basics down, and then I spend about half an hour to learn some tricks.

On the way to my parents, I feel like a kid again and can hardly wait to show my three fresh-learned Kongzhu tricks to them. Actually, Kongzhu does bring the inner child of me out, cheerful and agile. With the enjoyment and excitement of Kongzhu playing, I am young in spirit and playful at heart. (Dongmei Lu)

"Balancing the scale," a trick that a beginner can learn quickly

Kongzhu on a "chicken wire"

Jumping on and off the wire. She can do this sequence multiple times as long as the Kongzhu is spinning

"Looking at the moon in a clear sky"

"Come and play with us!"

Making it happen, kids are eager to learn at the Kongzhu corner in *Purple Bamboo Park*.

Lu Ding, 8, can play many tricks artfully. He channels his excessive energy after homework into some creative challenges.

Inviting Kongzhu onto Ice

In a winter morning, the big ice-covered lake in *Yuyuantan Park* becomes a playground for this gentleman who carefully lays the Kongzhu on ice after getting it spinning on the string, then he enjoys the amusement of spinning Kongzhu on ice.

WANT A NEW CHALLENGE?
Ms. Liu practices double Kongzhus in *Beihai Park*.

PASSION PAYS OFF
Mr. Li, 76, an ardent Kongzhu player, is so absorbed in the business of Kongzhu playing. Day after day and week after week, the untamed Kongzhu finally gets submissive under Mr. Li's perseverance.

"I sleep much better than before ever since I started playing Kongzhu a year ago," says Mr. Yu, 70. Kongzhu playing has become an integral part of Mr. Yu's self-preventive and self-recovering program for improving his health condition. He also pays attention to good-eating habits and maintains an easy-going attitude.

Forget about the sticks

Mr. Cai gets closer to Kongzhu by manipulating the string directly. In this way, he enjoys a much better workout and satisfaction.

Let the Passion Fuel the Motion

Use the sticks his way

Breaking off from the traditional way of playing, Mr. Sun, 71, makes retractable fiberglass-fishing poles a pair of Kongzhu sticks. "To me, Kongzhu is the most interesting game among all the games I enjoy."

Dancing with Kongzhu

Some passionate Kongzhu players can really move their bodies from head to toe. Different styles of ballroom dancing can be used to describe different styles of Kongzhu movements.

Shall we tango?

With his sudden leg-kicking and body-swinging, Mr. Cai (above) carefully leads his partner, Kongzhu, to the left and the right, front and back, under and above.

Let's waltz

With the graceful circular motion, Mr. Sun (below) is more like a waltz dancer. The even rhythm, the gentle steps, and the calming attitude make him an excellent waltz lead.

2.2 Shuttlecock Kicking (Hacky Sac)

踢
毽
子

Mr. An shows his balance, agility and artistry in *Jingshan Park*.

About Shuttlecock (Hacky Sac)

DESCRIPTION:

Shuttlecock is a traditional Chinese folk toy called Jianzi which means feathery arrow. Kicking the shuttlecock is like the American game "Hacky Sac."

HISTORY:

Chinese historical records show its origin as far back as the Han Dynasty (206 BC-220 AD). It became a popular folk-game during the Tang Dynasty (618-907), when shops specializing in shuttlecocks appeared. In the Ming Dynasty (1368-1644), formal competition of shuttlecock kicking was held. Shuttlecock kicking reached its peak in the Qing Dynasty (1616-1911), in terms of both crafting techniques and kicking skills. There were times in history when the game went in hibernation, but today it is fully awake, showing its vitality and longevity.

A winter-morning kicking session in *Yuyuantan Park*, a good warm-up for the whole day

Mr. Zhu (center) shows his genuine laugh.

Mr. Han practices while waiting for the regular members to arrive at *Jingshan Park*.

Shuttlecock - The Catalyst of Laughs
A Story of the Regulars in Jingshan Park

Who would know that a little feather toy can produce so many good laughs for those who love to chase and kick it. Not until you join a shuttlecock-kicking group, will you realize how powerful the toy can be as the catalyst of laughter.

The regular players are a group of easy-going retirees who are connected by a common object, the shuttlecock and who are adhered by the magic glue, good laughs.

The Queen of the Feather Ball

At the foot of the hill in *Jingshan Park*, there is a nice shaded area where the regular shuttlecock players meet every morning.

Among them there is a lady who stands out. She dresses beautifully as if she is on a stage for a fashion show and her face glows as if she is in her teens. Her waist twists gracefully to collaborate with the leg that lifts to the left and right and front and back to kick the feather ball.

She is Ms. Gu, 76, who has taken a bus to come to *Jingshan park* every morning for the last three years.

She always gets complements from people for her youthful look, fit body and good humor as well as her kicking skills.

"I like to wear pretty dresses and I like to laugh a lot," says she. Yes, her optimistic attitude and playful heart make her look beautiful and young and her daily kicking routine keeps her healthy.

Kicking with grace and playing with ease

Ms. Gu looks good, feels good and demonstrates that a good life is ageless.

Life Circle

After raising her kids and helping raise her grand kids, Ms. Gu becomes a kid herself who likes to play, but this time the impact of playing is far greater physically and mentally than before: To be self-reliant.

Ms. Gu enjoys a good laugh with her morning kicking group.

2.3 Kite Flying

About Kite

DESCRIPTION:

Feng Zheng is the Chinese for kite, which means "*wind harp*", a reference to the fact that kites were equipped with whistles and capable of making musical sound. Kite flying is a traditional Chinese pastime with millions of flyers across the nation.

Traditionally it is made of bamboo strip as the backbones and frames and paper or silk as covering. Today kite making can be so elaborate in techniques and materials.

There are unlimited shapes due to different culture and customs from different regions. The Chinese kites are rich in designs whose characteristics have close connection with local culture and craftsmanship. The mini-kite is smaller than a regular size of palm and the large one can be as big as a house. The longest kite can be as long as a hundred meters. (Source: www.chinaculture.org.)

HISTORY:

It first appeared in China about 2,000 years ago and was used for military purposes. Not until the Tang Dynasty (618-907) and the Song Dynasty (960-1279), did it start to become a popular pastime for common people. After the Ming Dynasty (1368-1644), kite flying gradually formed a "kite culture" and became a seasonal event around spring time. Today kite flying becomes more and more sophisticated and professional due to the level of difficulty and the large scale of kite design and making. But for the majority of folk who just like to have a good time when winds are rolling, a simple kite will do wonders for them.

WEIFANG KITE-MUSEUM

It is the traditional "Kite City" in Shandong province, China. It has the largest kite museum in the world and it hosts the famous Weifang International Kite Festival each April.

For more information on kites, visit the Weifang kite-museum website at www.wfkitemuseum.com.

The kite was the most important scientific device to have come to Europe from China.

—Joseph Needham (British scholar 1900-1995), *Science and Civilization in China*

When the Wind is Right

Flying a kite sometimes can be intimidating, but the right wind will provide loft for a properly equipped kite even for a beginner.

On the way to a local canal to accompany my mom for a Buddhist ritual event called the "fish-let-go ceremony," I can't help but notice all the kites above us. My attention goes to a long centipede made of 30 faces in series of the monkey king (a Chinese folklore hero). "May I try it?" I ask the street vendor. "Here you go," he hands it to me. Wow, I realize my childhood dream - some day I will fly a kite as high as that of the boys next door.

Here I am, several decades later, holding the impressive long kite and showing off in front of the camera. I too, can fly a kite when the wind is right.
(Dongmei Lu)

Kites make kids run and cheer.

A steady wind is needed to fuel the engine of this goldfish for a successful take-off. A morning in *Chaoyang Park*.

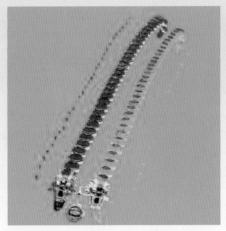

"Double dragons frolicking with the pearl," a kite designed according to a Chinese folklore legend. This is a good example of how kite-design is influenced by history, culture and tradition of each region or country.

A kite shop located in Nan-he-yan Street

Kite-flying makes a good family outing on weekends.

Tian'anmen Square - a Traditional Place for Kite Flying

Walking toward Tian'anmen Square from a distance can be intriguing. Before you see the square, you will be welcomed by numerous kites dancing in the sky.

If you are a kite lover, this is the right place to come, especially during the spring and fall seasons due to the favorable winds.

The Rare Treasures of Beijing

A folk painting "Wild with Joy" by folk artists from *Yangliuqing* over 100 years ago depicts how kids enjoyed outdoor play to their fullest when there were no electronic games or Internet.

These games shown in this chapter were popular during the 1940s and 50s especially among boys. Today the tradition is carried by adults who used to play these games in the old alleys and open spaces.

3.1 Juggling the Flower Stick

3.2 Spinning the Top

3.3 Snapping the Whip

3.4 Clapping the Bamboo Clapper

3.5 Rolling the Hoop

3.6 Shooting the Meteor Hammer

3.1 Juggling the Flower Stick

打
花
棍

About the Flower Stick

DESCRIPTION:
A player holds two wooden sticks about two-feet long as clubs and beat a third one. Since the object being juggled (beaten) is dressed up with colorful flowering tassels at both ends, the name of the game is "juggling the flower stick."

HISTORY:
People say this game started long ago among Chinese minority Li (one of the 55 minority groups resides in south China), as a dating-or-matchmaking game. Now it has grown out of the Li village into many parks in Beijing to become a recreational-fitness activity.

TECHNIQUE:
Rotating, turning, tossing and catching.... There are about ten-basic techniques one can learn. Getting the flower stick bouncing between the two clubs may take a couple of minutes, but to maintain a good control and to be able to do all the tricks might take weeks, months, even years. Like everything else, practice makes it perfect.

BENEFITS:
Many game players express that playing the game not only helps them move their whole bodies but also stimulates the brains because intense hand-eye coordination provides excitement as well as a workout.

Mr. Tian adds kicking to the juggling. *Temple of Heaven Park*

A Wake-up Call from a Back Injury

An unexpected lower-back pain several years ago changed Mr. Tian's lifestyle from juggling stressful daily life to juggling the playful flower stick.

One morning a sharp pain struck Mr. Tian as he was putting his socks on by the edge of the bed. He said that at that moment, a thought crossed to his mind: His lack of physical activity over the years had led him to what happened that day and it was time to get proactive toward his health. Meanwhile it took him more than a month to recover from the pain. But this negative incident has brought some positive outcome to Mr. Tian. Since then he has been hooked on the game of juggling the flower stick for the last three year.

"Playing the game makes me happy and the sticks have beaten the ailment and illness away. Now I'm disease free."

Today Mr. Tian is the leading force in populating the game in many parks in Beijing.

Rotating

Tossing

Catching

A Playful Path

Mr. Shi, 71, plays his way to *Jingshan Park* from his home nearby.

Talent has no limit

Ms. Wang, the Kongzhu teacher (see Chapter 2) also knows how to juggle the flower stick, how to perform Taiji sword and dance with the handkerchief. Her versatility inspires others to discover their own talent.

3.2 Spinning the Top

About Top-Spin

DESCRIPTION:
A bell-shaped wooden toy spins on the floor when it is whipped by a player. It is rather an old-fashioned toy.

HISTORY:
One unearthed top made of clay was found on the archaeological site in Xia County of Shanxi Province, China. It is said to be a Neolithic product. It became a popular folk toy during the Ming Dynasty (1368-1644).

MATERIAL:
A typical top has a flat-circular surface of two-to-three inches in diameter on the top and steel ball (for spinning) on the tip at the bottom. The whip is made of a foot-long wooden stick with about a two-foot-long rope tied to one end of it. As time progresses, different materials are being used.

SHAPE AND SIZE:
The shape is pretty consistent - just different belled shapes - but the size crosses a big range from a mini-version weighing only a few grams to giant ones that weigh up to about 100 kg.

TECHNIQUES:
One uses the whip as a launching string by wrapping it around the top many times and then setting the top in motion by flinging it to the floor and pulling the whip at the same time. Whip the top occasionally in order to maintain the spin.

BENEFITS:
It is a fun-filled folk game and a good outdoor activity that provides a simple and wholesome enjoyment and good workout for the shoulder, arm and heart.

A gentleman spins the top at the playground of *Taoranting Park*.

In the *Capital Museum*, a staff member is telling stories about some of the folk toys including the top.

Tops lighted by LEDs on the square in front of the *Beijing Exhibition Center*

3.3 Snapping the Whip

About the Whip-snap

DESCRIPTION:
A long whip is used for a physical workout by snapping it in the air.

HISTORY:
It is said that whip-snapping was used in the ceremony of welcoming state quests in Zhou Dynasty (1046-256 B.C.) and later as a traditional performance in a circus troupe.

MATERIAL:
The traditional whip is made of leather. For self entertainment and physical improvement, people in parks usually use less expensive material for the whip such as recycled inner tubes from vehicles.

WEIGHT AND SIZE:
It weighs about 3 pounds plus and is about 4 meters long.

TECHNIQUES:
Part your feet shoulder width, then (for the right- handed) raise your hand above the shoulder and go behind the head, then circle to the front and at the same time turn the wrist clockwise (circle above the head) to snap the whip. The power should originate from the waist and hip area and then the energy travels upward all the way to the tip of the whip through the arm.

BENEFITS:
It strengthens the muscles and joints around the shoulder, neck and lower back areas, hence regular practice can be a good therapy for alleviating pain around these areas.

A successful snap can be as loud as a firecracker.

Mr. Ren (top) and Mr. Zhao are practicing in *Temple of Heaven Park*.

3.4 Clapping the Bamboo

About the Bamboo Clapper

DESCRIPTION:
The player claps two sets of bamboo blocks, one in each hand, to make rhythmic sound. One set of the clappers is made of two blocks linked by a piece of red cloth and the other is made of a stack of five smaller blocks. A tactful collaboration between the two hands can make the clapping sound crisp and attractive.

HISTORY:
Traditionally, bamboo clappers are used to accompany story-telling for street-show business and performing on stage.

BENEFITS:
The left-and-right hand coordination helps to increase the sharpness of the brain. Of course, the practice will strengthen the wrists, arms, and shoulders. Today learning to clap bamboo blocks has become a pastime for folks who just enjoy making the perfect sprightly sound.

Mr. Zhang, 64, claps the bamboo in *Beihai Park* before he plays in a harmonica band. He has been playing with this instrument for twenty years.

Mr. Zhao used to be a short-distance runner who went to the International Amateur Field Games in London in 1999 when he was 45. Due to a leg injury, he opts for the bamboo clapping. "It helps improve my cognitive performance by working the left and right hands together to produce harmonious rhythms," says he.

Like other accompaniment instruments, the bamboo clapper provides unique percussion sound to spice up the harmonica band in *Purple Bamboo Park*.

3.5 Rolling the Hoop

About the Hoop-Rolling

DESCRIPTION:
Rolling the hoop is a traditional children's toy. An iron hoop (about 16 in diameter) is pushed by an iron hook (about two-feet long) handled by a player.

HISTORY:
It was a popular alley toy especially among boys during the 1940s, 50s and even 60s when there were no electronic games and Internet.

TECHNIQUES:
The basic technique is to roll it forward in a straight line. The next technique is to roll it in a circle. The trick is to control the hook to guide the hoop.

Mr. Liu, 74, brings his childhood toys - the iron hoops to *Beihai Park* and attracts many grownups with young hearts.

The hoop brings strangers together to relish their childhood memories. Notice that there are a few small rings circling the hoop which can make some pretty ringing sound when the hoop rolls.

A woman can not resist her childhood toy and wants to go back in time when pushing the hoop and running along with the boys in the neighborhood alley brought her so much excitement and fun.

3.6 Shooting the Meteor Hammer

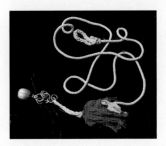

About the Meteor Hammer

DESCRIPTION:
The meteor hammer is one of the soft weapons in the Chinese martial-art family.
It is made of a fifteen-foot-long rope and solid copper ball as big as an egg and
shaped like a papaya which acts like a little hammer. The connection between
the rope and the copper hammer is a little ring or rings. The copper is wrapped
in a piece of red silk. When it is flung into the air, it is just like a meteor shooting
across the dark sky.

HISTORY:
It can be traced to ancient times when people use it (vine-and-rock version) for
hunting.

TECHNIQUE:
One can skillfully integrate the techniques of winding, turning, throwing to
perform a sequence of movements such as tying the rope around one's neck,
chest, waist, arms, legs, or feet without getting hurt. To get oneself off the rope,
one has to let the hammer go fast like a shooting meteor. For a beginner, a little
sandbag can be used to replace the metal hammer.

BENEFITS:
This whole body workout can enhance one's strength, flexibility and agility as
well as reaction time.

Mr. Wang, 71, is shooting the meteor without hitting himself and that is the art of control.
He often gets requests for teaching the game by onlookers. *Temple of Heaven Park*

Classic-Leisure Scenes in Beijing

This traditional entrance to a courtyard of a Beijing residence no longer exists. It was torn down in 2002.

When the "birdman" is out, the restaurant is open. A restaurant promotes its Beijing-style food with the flavor of old Beijing reflected by this old fashioned gentleman.

Today as more and more old neighborhoods are replaced by apartment buildings, classic old-neighborhood leisure pursuits are moving to parks and new community centers.

Parks and public areas play important roles in people's lives for pleasure and relaxation since the majority of people live in tight apartment buildings in urban areas of Beijing.

4.1 Bird-Cage Walking

4.2 Chess and Card Playing

4.3 Chatting

4.1 Bird-cage Walking

遛鸟

Two bird fanciers in the neighborhood of *Shichahai Lake*

Mr. Zhao brings his birds along when he goes swimming in the lake at the *Yuyuantan Park*.

Bird Fanciers

Today it would be hilarious if a woman carries a bird-case in public, but it is quite common to see men usually middle-aged or older strolling around their neighborhoods, on streets, or in parks with birdcages in their hands. Being accompanied by the birds, they look content and satisfied.

Bird walking doesn't stop them from pursuing other pleasures such as reading, swimming, chatting, dancing, singing and the list is endless. As long as the birds are nearby and comfortable, the owners will be happy to share a good time with them out in nature, basking in the sun.

The bird is watching its owner dancing in *Taoranting Park*.

 **Hill Myna - A TALKING BIRD -** is a resident of the hill regions of South Asia. In China, the bird can be found in Yunnan, Guangxi and Hainan. Treasured for its ability to mimic the human voice and other sounds, this simple black bird not only enjoys its popularity among bird fanciers but also from many admirers who happen to hear its parroting of humans in parks or streets.

Happy Together

"Eat first, and then talk," the bird demands in Chinese to his master - Mr. Li, who takes care of his bird like his little kid and hands the bird a treat. Then the bird starts to talk with a high pitched voice. "You look beautiful," says the bird in Chinese and "apple" in English and some other random words or phrases.

Soon Mr. Li is joined by two more regular birding friends who have the same kind of bird. They hang their cages one next to another, then they start to share some tips for raising the birds while listening to the birds talking.

"The moon casts light through the window
And illuminates the floor with white light like a layer of frost.
I raise my head looking at the moon,
And drop my head thinking of my hometown,"
the bird recites a sentimental poem by a famous poet, Li Bai from the Tang Dynasty (618-907).
His voice is so crisp and clear. Mr. Li is very proud of him.

A morning walk in the *North Second-Ring-Road Sidewalk Park*
Walking with a cloth cover over the birdcage is said to prevent fright from sudden sound or movement outside the cage; rocking the birdcage helps birds strengthen their grabs to the cage.

At Ease

Out and about, Mr. Ma is basking in the early morning sunshine at the roadside between the *Forbidden City* and the *Jingshan Park*. Sitting next to him on the tricycle are his outing companions - birds in the two cloth-covered cages. "I'm just strolling around and taking it easy." His other pleasures are fishing, flying whistling pigeons and playing Chinese chess.

His old fashioned clothes appear comfortable just as the look on his face does.

He takes out some homemade pancakes from the compartment under the birdcages and starts his breakfast picnic while observing the world passing by.

At age 90, he has seen a lot, from the old Beijing which came out of the Qing Dynasty (1616-1911) to today's Beijing in the beginning of the 21st century. Watching the world around him changing rapidly he knows one thing remains unchanged - his peaceful state of mind, which has helped him going through rough times as well as good times, an under-looked yet profound factor in prolonging life.

4.2 Chess and Card Playing

棋
牌

Two gentlemen in *Temple* of *Heaven Park*

About Chinese Chess

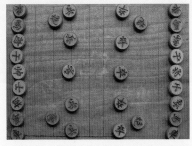

The board setup

DESCRIPTION:
As in Western chess, there are sixteen pieces per side but the pieces are inscribed with the function of the individual piece like Soldier, General, Horse, Chariot and so on. It moves faster than Western chess does because it is more tactical and less strategic.

HISTORY:
A form existed in the Zhanguo period (475-221 B.C.). Chinese chess since the Song Dynasty (960-1279) has not changed much.

On a street corner, these regular chess players always attract passing-by spectators who enjoy watching as much as offering advice and making comments.

The hectic street doesn't seem to bother these two easy-going players.

About Card Playing

Invented around 2,000 years ago for soldiers' recreation during wartime, today the ancient Chinese cards have lost their popularity to the Western cards, especially in public recreation domain.

Western cards came to China around Opium War (1840). And the Chinese name for porker is "puke".

Unlike Chinese chess playing, card playing can be seen among both genders in public sight.

Along the corridor of the *Temple of Heaven Park*, there are many groups of card and chess players.

Ladies are helping themselves with some "card" time in the morning before the restaurant opens.
Shichahai Lake

4.3 Chatting

Chatting is a necessity in the lives of Chinese as seeing psychiatrists is not common in society. Neighbors, friends, or people with similar background get together sharing their stories, exchanging experiences, or educating each other about new things. Anyway, it is a healthy pastime for reducing loneliness, channeling emotions, and enriching each other's mind.

Yuyuantan Park

North Second-Ring-Road Sidewalk Park

Chatting along the lake in *Yuyuantan Park*

New Inventions of Fun

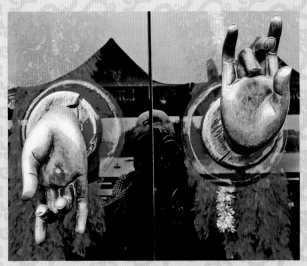

A pair of door handles made of Buddha hands

Open the door to creativity.
Be inspired and be inspiring.

5.1 Ground Calligraphy

5.2 Clapping-and-Chanting Drill

5.3 Ring Tossing

5.4 Taiji-Soft Ball

5.1 Ground Calligraphy

地书

A man is practicing in *Changpuhe Park*

About the Ground Calligraphy

Many practitioners bring their water jars to wet brushes.

DEFINITION:

The ground calligraphy is practiced on any paved, smooth, solid surface on the ground with a wet-sponge brush.

HISTORY:

Some practitioners say that around 1984, a gentleman regularly practiced calligraphy on a sidewalk along an overpass, using a stick with cotton (later advanced to sponge) bonded to its end as a brush, water as ink and concrete ground as paper. Onlookers were fascinated and inspired. Before long, special brushes for this particular use were sold commercially and ground calligraphy was born. It rapidly became popular in the parks in Beijing.

ADVANTAGES:

There are two advantages that ground calligraphy has over conventional calligraphy. First, it eliminates the need for paper, ink, and expensive traditional hair-made brushes (the sponge-tipped brush can be easily made at home). Second, it gets people out in nature, where they can make friends, get free critics and learn from each other (since not many people own backyards of their own in Beijing).

A calligraphy supply store, in *Liulichang Street*, sells both kinds of brushes. The two big brushes, about three-foot long, hanging in front of the door are traditional ones used on paper; the two inside the door with pointed tips are used on ground - smooth pavement.

Traditional Scholar's
Four Treasures and Four Arts

文房四宝：笔、墨、纸、砚　　文人四艺：琴、棋、书、画

Paper, ink, brush, and ink-stone, these traditional calligraphy supplies are called the *Four Treasures of a Scholar's Study Room*.

Zither, board game, calligraphy, and painting are considered as the *Four Arts of Chinese Scholars*.

CHINESE CALLIGRAPHY

THE CULTURE:

Calligraphy is an important component of Chinese culture. It is an artistic expression of one's handwriting. Evolved over thousands of years, it has a close tie with Chinese painting, classic poems, literature and history. Traditionally, calligraphy is one of the *Four Arts of Chinese Scholars*. Today, studying and practicing calligraphy are part of the curriculum in most elementary schools.

FIVE MAIN SCRIPTS:

Seal, Clerical (Official), Regular, Semi-Cursive (Running), and Cursive (Grass). The five photos below are examples of the five main scripts listed in sequence from left to right accordingly.

THE ART OF THE BRUSH:

Brushes were invented as early as the Neolithic Age, about 5000 B. C. in China. Like traditional Chinese painting, calligraphy is another form of visual art. The springiness of the brush gives the Chinese characters endless expressions and unlimited style.

CALLIGRAPHY AND PAINTING:

Since painting and calligraphy share the same tools - paper, ink, and brush, the two are often integrated; in fact, after the Yuan dynasty (1206-1368), you hardly see a Chinese painting without calligraphy on it.

A section of a landscape painting called "Autumn"
by Zhao Mengfu from the Yuan Dynasty

Many masterpieces used poems as themes or added charm. These are known as "literati paintings" in which artists combined talents of calligraphy, poetry, and painting to further their artistic creations.

Calligraphy: Does Anybody Care?

The Benefits according to Mr. Shi

What's the big deal about calligraphy? Who cares if you practice it on paper or ground? Mr. Shi, 66, who has been a lifetime calligrapher and has been practicing ground calligraphy for the last three years, will tell you the answer.

CULTURAL GRATIFICATION – You will be a better person for it.

It has been a long tradition that practicing calligraphy helps cultivate one's fine taste and appreciation of literature, philosophy and art in general. Mr. Shi feels proud that he has been engaged in this lifetime pursuit to manifest his moral character from the nourishment of reciting so many great ancient works that are full of wisdom and inspiration.

MENTAL FITNESS – You will improve the memory for it.

Mr. Shi's daily ground calligraphy ritual consists of reciting the 320-word "Preface to the Orchid Pavilion Collection," a prominent piece in the history of Chinese calligraphy, written by Wang Xizhi (303-361) who is known as the "Sage of Calligraphy" from the Eastern Jin Dynasty. Mr. Shi spends about twenty-five minutes each morning to write these 320 words from his memory in the Semi-Cursive script that Wang Xizhi used in the piece. Then, he will spend some time reciting some classic poems from the Tang or Song dynasties.

PHYSICAL IMPROVEMENT – You will be challenged by your coordination skills!

Practicing calligraphy has therapeutic effect. It's like practicing Taiji with a brush – the graceful and vigorous movements of the brush encourage a great deal of coordination. To master the art of ground calligraphy, a practitioner needs to coordinate a steady hand with a flexible wrist and strong arm with pliable elbow and malleable shoulder while walking backward to write one word after another.

EMOTIONAL CONNECTION – You will feel connected with nature and people.

What makes Mr. Shi excited every morning is the anticipation of going to the park where he can get inspiration by immersing himself in the beautiful surroundings – to be with nature and calligraphy friends.

No! They are not mopping the pavement; they are practicing ground calligraphy. It is often the first activity you see after you enter a park. *Tuanjiehu Park*

From Paper to Paved Ground

For more than two thousands years, calligraphy was considered an indoor-scholarly endeavor of common people who wanted to improve their social status, or it belonged to wealthy individuals, usually nobles, who wanted to develop literary or artistic tastes for their own pleasure.

Today, the idea of practicing calligraphy on paved ground opens a wider gate for those who want to enter the "palace" of calligraphy. Many people who might have been concerned about the cost of paper and ink feel relief from these costs. Also this outdoor activity provides a free-open-air classroom for the beginners to learn from the experienced ones.

What a "reservoir of ink!"

A gentleman practices ground calligraphy in *Linglong Park*. The pagoda is called *Linglong* or *Cishou Pagoda*.

Qi (Chi) and Calligraphy

The word "Qi" is often seen in connection with Taiji, Qigong, or traditional Chinese medicine in many Western illustrations. But in China, Qi is ubiquitous. Since Qi means the breath of life or energy circulating in one's body, without it there won't be life of any kind.

According to traditional Chinese medicine, free flow of Qi is vital to one's health. How to best collect, nourish, and clear Qi as well as how to best promote the circulation of Qi in one's body are constant concerns of those who believe in the importance of Qi to health.

As in the case of calligraphy, the free flow of Qi not only benefits one's brush strokes that lead to unrestrained calligraphy but also benefits the practitioner's health: practicing calligraphy is, in essence, practicing Qi. Therefore, it is very important to know how to cultivate Qi through mindfulness and how to flow Qi to the tip of the bush through the art of channeling Qi freely. This explains why a standing position is preferred when doing Chinese painting or calligraphy because Qi would be less likely to be blocked than that of in a sitting position.

Ground-calligraphy-brush seller in *Jingshan Park*. The brush costs about $2 each.

Youngsters are having fun with ground calligraphy, Sunday morning in *Taoranting Park*.

The peach symbolizes longevity. Mr. Wang incorporates the character **shou** - longevity, inside a peach.

Visual Art on Ground

The regular park-goers like to call him teacher Wang, an ardent ground calligrapher who shows up at the east entrance of the *Tuanjiehu Park* every morning to enjoy the pleasure of ground calligraphy. People who pass by the gate can't miss or ignore Mr. Wang's impressive skills in calligraphy.

His smooth and vigorous strokes of each character show confidence and sophistication as well as inner spirit.

Ground calligraphy moves the ancient visual art from paper on a scholar's desk to the public forum on the ground. It offers instant "exhibitions" that won't stay very long since the wet marks evaporate, but these exhibitions never end, for practicing ground calligraphy is a daily ritual of many residents.

Mr. Wang displays his artistic expression of the character **he** - crane, another symbol for long life.

In *Yuyuantan Park*, Mr. Yu, 76, is a regular ground calligrapher who uses his left hand to practice. He says in this way a different part of the brain gets an opportunity to be exercised and hence an overall improvement of the brain is expected.

A gentleman is practicing cursive style about half way to the top of the *Fragrant Hills*.

This gentleman's brush weighs over 5 pounds.

Beijing 2008 Olympics has a significant place in the Chinese's hearts. Zhang, 75, writes: "China realizes the dream of hosting the hundred-year Olympic Games."

5.2 Ring Tossing

乾
坤
圈

Wang Renquan, one of the two inventors
of the game would teach anybody who is
interested in learning.

About Ring Tossing

This new game is mostly seen in the northeast part of the *Temple of Heaven Park*. It was invented in 2002 by two men named Li Chuenman and Wang Renquan, both in their 70s. The two gentlemen turned discarded used-rubber pipes into colorful rings by covering them with soft fabric. As they tossed the rings to each other, they discovered that trying to catch the rings with different parts of the body especially with the head was fun and challenging.

The game became popular after it was reported on TV and in newspaper and has been spread to other parks and cities. It is a quick playful way to get a thorough workout for neck, shoulder, arm and spine.

"Go!" The lady tells the ring while tossing it to her partner in *Temple of Heaven Park*.

It is coming!

"Got it!"

5.3 Clapping-and-chanting Drill

About the Clapping-and-chanting Drill

DESCRIPTION:

Practitioners clap their hands or other parts of their bodies and chant positive, uplifting and comforting phrases to promote health. The practice is related to traditional Chinese medicine (TCM), including meridian stimulation and Qigong practice for improving one's general health conditions and relieving symptoms of diseases.

ORIGINATOR:

Ma Chengkai, a Qigong master and researcher from Beijing Wuming Life-and-Science and Health-Recovery Research Center, started publishing in 1996 a series of articles on theories and methods of "Clapping and Chanting" in the "China Qigong Science" magazine. Since then some beneficiaries of the practice pioneered the Clapping-and-Chanting Drill in *Temple of Heaven Park* every morning as a group activity. Now this group routine has spread into many parks in Beijing and other cities of China.

BENEFITS:

According to TCM, the ten fingers are connected to the nervous system and vital organs of the body via meridians. Clapping hands help stimulate the circulation of Qi, hence promote better health.

CAUTIONS:

For a beginner, start the practice with 5 to 15 minutes at a time, then gradually increase the time to a half hour. No practice is recommended at least one half hour before and after a meal, nor before bed time.

Qi, Meridians, and TCM

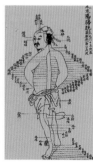

According to traditional Chinese medicine (TCM), Qi, life energy, flows through channels called meridians on the surface of a human body. There are 12 primary meridians, six Yin and six Yang, and each relates to one of the organs. There are 6 meridians going through the hand, 3 on each side of the hand. There are 360 primary acupuncture points along these meridians.

TCM states that imbalances in the flow of Qi cause illness. A comprehensive system of practices of TCM is designed to help people restore the balance. The practices include acupuncture, moxibustion, manipulative massage techniques such as Tuina and Guasha, herbal medicine, diet and lifestyle changes, meditation, and exercise (often in the form of *Qigong* or *Taiji*).

Books on TCM

McClellan, Sam. *Integrative Acupressure*. New York: The Berkley Publishing Group, 1998.

Beinfield, Harriet and Korngold, Efrem. *Between Heaven and Earth*. New York: The Ballantine Publishing Group, 1991.

Elias, Jason and Ketcham, Katherine. *Chinese Medicine for Maximum Immunity: Understanding the Five Elemental Types for Health and Well-Being*. New York: Three Rivers Press, 1999.

Dong, Paul and Esser, Aristide H. *Chi Gong: The Ancient Chinese Way to Health*. New York: Paragon House, 1990.

Clapping Everyday Keeps Doctor Away

"I was skeptical at first, and then I joined the clapping group thinking that it won't hurt to give it a try. A couple of months later, I was so surprised to see that the ten-year-long skin problem on my hands was gone," a lady in her 50s says in *Yuyuantan Park* where a regular hand-clapping group practice every morning.

"The special energy is just next to you,
    It clears the mind and channels through the body,"

"超常能量，就在身边，思维沟通，全身通畅"

The group of 50 plus people chants with strong and rhythmic voice while clapping.

They not only clap their hands together but also clap their bodies from head to toe. Many people are hooked on it due to the health benefits they have gained from it. Some say they have improved the quality of their sleep; some say they have reduced the three-highs: hypertension, high cholesterol, and high blood sugar as well as other chronic illness. Most people say that after the morning clapping-and-chanting drill, they feel stress-and-tension free for the rest of the day.

The regular clapping group in *Yuyuantan Park*

The regular clapping group in *Dragon Pool Park*

This soothing, meditative and therapeutic clapping-and-chanting drill comforts hundreds and thousands of people who find comfort in this simple way of feeling better.

5.4 Taiji-soft Ball

太极柔力球

Taiji-soft ball brings rhythm and grace to a game. A woman enjoys the game in *Temple of Heaven Park*.

About Taiji-soft Ball

DESCRIPTION:

Taiji-soft ball (Taiji Rouli-qiu in Chinese. Rouli means soft and vigorous, and qiu, ball) embodies Taiji philosophy - to maintain a dynamic balance between Yin and Yang energy. Players use the soft-and-gentle "Yin" approach toward the incoming ball which possesses "Yang" energy. Borrowing the "Yang" energy from the ball, players redirect the ball and let it go. All of the movements are like Taiji: supple, fluid, and graceful. The game can be played solo, in pairs, or in group.

HISTORY:

Wang Rong, a graduate from the Department of Physical Education of Shanxi University, created the game while teaching PE at the Jinzhong Health School in Shanxi in 1991. With a short history of ten-plus years, the game enjoys a fast growing popularity. It has not only spread all over China but also Japan.

MATERIAL:

The ball is made of a plastic shell with some sand inside causing it to cling to the racquet rather than spring off it. The racquet is like a tennis racquet except the net is made of a soft-synthetic-rubber sheet with small holes in it for air to go through. The soft and elastic surface of the racquet allows the sand-filled ball to stick to it easily while the player turns and swings the racquet in circular motion.

TECHNIQUES:

There are three essential techniques: retrieving, leading or redirecting, and letting go. All these movements should be happening continuously like Taiji movements.

BENEFITS:

Many players express that playing Taiji-soft ball has improved their cognitive and physical performance.

Juggling three balls between four racquets

1.Retrieving

2. Leading the balls
to a save position or
redirecting them

3. Letting them go with a
curve

Good Health is My Best Asset for Retirement

Mr. Li, now 65, retired at 60, has been teaching Taiji-soft ball in *Yuyantan Park* for the past four years every morning, rain or shine. From beginners to graduates, the number of his students over the last four years is probably in the hundreds.

Mr. Li is practicing with his students in *Yuyuantan Park*

"I could be rehired again by some other companies, but if my health is impaired by the stress of work, what can the extra money do for me? It will just go to the hospital. I'd rather take care of my health first in order to enjoy life. I prefer good health to money and good health is my best asset for my retirement. Now I want to share this asset with others," says Mr. Li. "From strangers to friends, we not only play Taiji-soft ball together, we also go hiking and sightseeing in the outskirts of Beijing. There were thirty-five of us who went to the *Beijing Botanical Garden* last week and had a picnic there. Our goal is to make sure that we are happy every day," he adds.

Non-Competition Sports

Sunset Swimmer (oil on canvas painting by Hongmei Lu)

6.1 Outdoor Gyms

6.2 Fishing

6.3 Swimming

6.4 Skating

6.5 Hiking

6.1 Outdoor Gyms

露天免费
健身器材

Li Rong-ao, five and one half, in *Tuanjiehu Park*

About Outdoor Gyms

While going to the membership gyms or fitness clubs is trendy among young people, using free outdoor gyms or fitness facilities is favored by the general public in Beijing.

Since 2001, these outdoor fitness centers have been installed in urban communities, public parks, squares, roadside, bus stops and other convenient locations by the government using sport lottery proceeds.

Fitness equipment can be therapeutic, such as these two:
one for shoulder rotating and the other for leg massaging.

A baby girl wants to walk on the treadmill

Grandma flies on the glider

Community and park playground

The fitness center in *Yuyuantan Park*

Ms. Wang likes to become good with all of the equipments.

The Outdoor Gym in Tuanjiehu Park

"Don't go yet. There will be talented people soon to do their daily practices," Ms. Wang (see the two photos above) tells me. And I am glad that I didn't leave and had the opportunity to take these photos of people who could do some amazing gymnastic routines. Ms. Wang herself likes to try all of the facilities and enjoys the progress she has been making everyday. "I just like to show myself that I can do what others can do." (Dongmei Lu)

Horizontal.
Mr. Tao has the strength and balance like a gymnast.

Vertical.
People are serious and diligent about using these facilities which are modified for amateur practices.

Abacus, a good brain-exercise device, is more attractive when it is on the playground.

Standing on the rotating saucers, the three users are having a good waist-twisting time.

6.2 Fishing

钓
鱼

Fishing in the "moon". *Purple Bamboo Park*

Shichahai Lake changes from an ice-skating rink in winter to a fishing pond and swimming pool in other seasons.

6.3 Swimming

"Come on in, the water is fine 365 days a year."
—A regular swimmer in *Yuyuantan Park*

Common Swimming Spots in *Yuyuantan Park*

Stars ★ indicate the favorite spots for swimmers in *Yuyuantan park*.
The map made of ceramic tiles is located at the east gate of the park.

About Winter Swimming

DEFINITION OF WINTER SWIMMING:
The weather temperature is below 0 °C (32 °F) while the outdoor-water temperature is below 14 °C (57.2 °F).

MAIN BENEFITS:
Boosting the immune system and improving the respiratory and circulatory systems.

FACTS:
There are about 3000 winter swimmers in Beijing. Most of them are retirees. Around 100 people are members of the East Lake Swimming Team of *Yuyantan Park*, nearly 30 of them women. For many of the winter swimmers, swimming is a daily ritual.

A TIP FOR BECOMING A WINTER SWIMMER:
"Start from summer next year and join us every day, then you can be a winter swimmer too," a regular swimmer says.

Source: *Beijing Winter Swimming* Magazine, October, 2005.

Winter swimmers in *Yuyuantan Park*

Winter Swimming in *Yuyuantan Park*

Feb 9th, 2006, around 7:30 a.m., the weather temperature is -12 °C (10.4 °F) and the water, 1 °C (33.8 °F).

After swimming in the icy lake, swimmers like to use a bottle of warm water to rinse off the chill.

Mr. Zhang, 84, has enjoyed winter swimming for the last thirteen years. He says that regular swimming has kept diseases away from him.

The regular swimmers share their icy pleasures in *Yuyuantan Park*.

This Pool of Water Saved My Life

A Story from Ms. Da-he

Suffering from asthma attacks for more than 30 years, Ms. Da-he, 71, knows how wonderful life is without it.

From this pool, carved out of a sheet of ice, she began a journey to rid herself of the misery of asthma 24 years ago.

After she learned that winter swimming could cure arthritis and other chronic diseases, she wanted to give it a try for alleviating her asthma. She started swimming in the spring of 1982, and continued through summer and fall, finally eased into the winter. The water was freezing cold, but she steeled herself and did not quit. Only one year had passed but her symptoms were gone and her new life without asthma had begun. Since then, Ms. Da-he gained a special affection for the water that she couldn't live without. "I am always thinking of this pool of water," she says with a grateful voice. "This pool of water saved my life," Ms. Da-he tells her story to those who are impressed by her strength and courage; she inspires them to take the plunge to a healthier and better life.

Winter

The morning was cold, -12 °C (10.4 °F) and the water in the lake, 1 °C (33.8 °F). Along the east bank of the lake in *Yuyuantan Park*, there were many groups of people, some of them were breaking the ice and some of them were in the water. They are the fearless winter swimmers. Among them, there was a lady who had just stepped out of the icy lake with icicles decorating her short hair and she was laughing and chatting with her swimming friends. "Call me Da-he and everybody here knows Da-he," she introduced herself to us who were so impressed by her ability to swim in such cold water. Ms. Da-he was a warm and friendly lady and her story of how winter swim helped her overcome asthma was really inspiring. "People used to call me 'the breather' and now thanks to this pool of water, I'm free of the heavy gasping and I can breathe like a normal person."

Spring

The second time we met Da-he was in May. Around the same time of day and around the same spot, I asked a lady who just finished swimming if she saw Da-he this morning. "She is over there," the lady pointed to the middle of the lake. We were so excited to see Da-he again. This time she was wearing a yellow swimsuit and she was happy to see us, too. She always seems in a good spirit and likes to laugh and talk a lot. Besides swimming, she told us, she likes hiking in the suburbs of Beijing.

Autumn

In September, we saw Da-he the third time. It seemed that she looked younger and younger each time we saw her. We guess the secret must be in the water.

This is where I learned how to swim, from this rock.

Ms. Wang is doing some warm-up before she gets on the rock for her jump start.

"Swimming makes me happy. The water washes all my worries and stress away and pours good energy into my body." Ms. Wang, 64, just learned swimming four years ago and now she swims like an Olympic star.

Immersed in the water, she finds peace and tranquility

A Story from Ms. Wang

Jumping into the water is her way to temporarily escape from the everyday mundane. The lake provides a sanctuary for her to be in solitude.

Ms. Wang has a lot to cope with at home. In addition to her own poor health, she has a family illness with which to deal. Worries and stress toward her loved one had made her health worse and she cried and cried many times quietly to release her fear and sorrow. But ever since she started swimming every morning, she has found a great way to relieve herself from all the emotional baggage she has carried on her shoulders. "Once I'm in the water, my mind goes blank. It is a beautiful feeling," she describes. "And that helps me boost my positive strength in life." That positive strength has gradually shown in her mental and physical improvement. "I feel much stronger now."

"The water reminds us that life is so beautiful and we ought to be optimistic and make the best out of it," says Ms. Wang.

Singing While Swimming

A Story from Mr. Big Wolf

If you happen to be strolling along the bank of the lake in *Yuyuantan Park* in the morning, you might hear beautiful Chinese folk songs or romantic Russian tunes lingering across the water. That must be the well-known singer-swimmer Mr. Big Wolf (nickname by fellow swimmers). "By the time I finish swimming and get to the bank, I probably have sung ten songs," he chats with people while he gets dry and dressed. No, he is not done, yet. While he is drying and putting clothes on he is still singing. It is said that both singing and swimming are good for improving the lung capacity. To Mr. Big Wolf who makes his trip here by a long bike ride weekly, singing and swimming are just two of his pleasures which happen to mix together naturally to enhance his mood. His other pleasures include biking every week to Ming Tombs, a famous scenic area located about 50 kilometers northwest of the center of Beijing, and eating some steamed meat buns cooked in a bamboo steamer at his favorite places on the way there or back.

Local people prefer lakes or canals to pubic pools for swimming.

Shichahai Lake in May

6.4 Skating

Families and friends on *Shichahai Lake*

Beijing's winter offers great outdoor ice-skating places in many parks like *Beihai Park*, *Summer Palace,* and *Shichahai Lake*.
Skating rental concessions charge about ¥10 ($1.25) per day.
Sleds are even more popular in winter. They rent for ¥5 (about 60¢) per hour.

6.5 Hiking

A path to Senyuhu Pavilion in fall. *Fragrant Hills Park*

Western Hills range is about 20 kilometers away from the city center
(photo taken from the peak of the Vista Hill, *Jingshan Park*).

About the Western Hills Range

The center of Beijing is flat. If you see any hills in the city, they are probably ornamental ones designed for parks such as *Beihai* and *Jingshan*.

The *Western Hills* range, part of the *Taihang* mountain range, houses many well-known historical mountainous parks like *Fragrant Hills*, *Badachu*, *Fenghuang Ling*, and *Baiwangshan*.

Besides their natural beauties, these parks are rich in cultural relics. Ancient pagodas, pavilions, temples and gardens blend in with the streams, lakes, and forested hills, providing an ideal hiking environment for many city dwellers.

Climbing the Scenic *Fragrant Hills*

Situated at the tail end of the larger *Western Hills* range, *Fragrant Hills Park* is famous for its red leaves in autumn. Established in 1186 as an imperial retreat, the forest park covers 160 hectares (about 395 acres) and consists of twenty-eight scenic spots. Climbers can reach an elevation of 557 meters (about 1,800 feet) on the main peak - Xianglu (the fragrant incense burner) Peak where they can have a panoramic view of the city to the east.

It is like a ritual for the locals to hike up the *Fragrant Hills* regularly.

A group of young people on the peak of the *Fragrant Hills*

The Regulars of the Fragrant Hills Park

Date: July 15th, 2006, around 9:30 am.
Temperature: 33 °C (91.4 °F) and humid.
The story: This gentleman, in his 70's, is a regular climber who comes here with fully equipped climbing gear - a straw hat, a radio hanging around his neck, a walking stick, a fan and a face towel in his backpack, a lunch box, and a bottle of water.
He says: "I live in the east part of the city and it takes me nearly two hours to come here by bus, so I only come two or three times a week. My lunch? I made some dumplings last night. Later on I will find myself a nice quiet place to enjoy them. Regular hiking helps me stay healthy and independent. I really want to maintain my health, so I don't have to rely on my kids."

Date: same as above.
Who: The two hikers, one 76 (left) and the other 83.
They say:"We live nearby, so we come here everyday. Among the daily climbers, we are not really old. There is a 92-year-old lady who hikes much faster than we do. It's no good to sit in an air-conditioned room in a hot day like this. You need to sweat a bit and this is the best place to do so because of the high oxygen content in this forestry area."

Jingshan Park

Jingshan means the Vista Hill. It was a part of the imperial palace of the Yuan Dynasty and an imperial garden during the Ming and Qing Dynasties. Since it lies on the central axis of the city, right behind *Forbidden City*, and it is the highest point in the center of the city, it is an ideal spot for overlooking the golden-roof *Forbidden City* to the south, the stunning sunset behind the giant White Pagoda in the *Beihai Park* to the west and the beautiful *Drum Tower* to the north.

Looking at *Jingshan Park* across the lake in *Beihai Park*

A Day off from Climbing

A Story from Mr. Rong

Mr. Rong, 82, climbs briskly on steep rock steps as if he were walking on a flat pathway in *Jingshan Park*. It takes no time for him to return to this midpoint from the top. "I'm taking a break today. Instead of climbing a real mountain, I'm climbing this hill for a break," says Mr. Rong, who is addicted to mountain climbing. He considers that climbing a small hill is a day off from climbing big mountains like *Fenghuang Ling* (Phoenix Mountain Range), Baiwangshan, or Badachu located along the Western Hills range.

"Once, I was climbing *Fenghuang Ling* and I saw a group of college kids debating whether to go higher since they were scared of the steep slope. I told them to follow me. I knew a route that was easier to get them to the top." He is so proud of himself for knowing so many places to go climbing. He has an annual pass (see the red badge on his pants) for most of major parks in Beijing (the annual pass for retirees over 65 costs ¥50, about $8).

Mr. Rong embodies the saying: "Early to bed and early to

Mr. Rong is at the midpoint of the hill in *Jingshan Park*.

rise makes a man healthy, wealthy and wise." Getting up around 4:00 a.m. everyday and going to bed around 8:30 p.m., he fills his day with a lot of activities. He likes to take buses everywhere to revisit some memorable places or to explore some new places to climb. The pride he exhibits while talking about his climbing accomplishments is only exceeded by the enthusiasm he has for finding new heights to conquer. He is, indeed, wealthy with good health and precious wisdom.

7

Let's Dance

Local residents in *Purple Bamboo Park* on May Day

One of the traditional dance themes is to celebrate a good harvest. Most of the time people dance just to express their inner spirit of love and passion for life.

7.1 Yang-ge

7.2 Fan Dance

7.3 Folk Dance

7.4 Ballroom Dance

7.5 Free Style

7.6 Ribbon Dance

7.1 Yang-ge

"Happily Ever After (retirement) Yang-ge Team", ages from 40s to 80s, at a community Yang-ge event.

About Yang-ge

Yang-ge is a popular rural folk dance which is all about excitement, energy and the spirit of celebration. Yang-ge means the song of rice seeding. This century-old art form has many distinctive local flavors or styles from various regions of China for celebrating farming related occasions like the Spring Festival, harvest and a range of folklore fairs.

Today the traditional Yang-ge has become a daily recreational street-or-square dance in Beijing. Usually ladies dress up in colorful costumes and do a four-step march while waving fans or handkerchiefs to the beat of drums, gongs, and cymbals played by a group of gentlemen.

The combination of sound, color, and exuberant movements creates an exciting and joyful atmosphere which makes Yang-ge one of the signature pleasures of Beijing.

The *Happily Ever After* (retirement) *Yang-ge Team*, percussion group

Meet the Musicians Who Set the Beat for Yang-ge

A big drum is a must for setting the beat; gongs, cymbals and Suona (a high-pitched trumpet) add more excitement to the rhythm.

The gentlemen on *Honglian Square*

It takes place in the mornings under an overpass.

It takes place at the nights on a square or along a street.

It takes place everywhere, everyday.

The Yang-ge King

Yang-ge Chen is an enthusiastic Yang-ge dancer and a cymbal player on the square of *Beijing Exhibition Center*. He starts his night with cymbal playing for the Yang-ge parade and then jumps into the Yang-ge march to enjoy what he is really fond of. His authentic moves make him a star among the ladies. He collects Yang-ge VCDs and DVDs from different regions of different styles. At age of 80, Mr. Chen is going strong. "Yang-ge keeps me young and happy," says Mr. Chen.

7.2 Fan Dance

Fan Dancers in *Beihai Park*

About Fan Dance

Fan dance is a hybrid between Yang-ge and contemporary folk dance. Instead of drums, folk music and popular songs are used as accompaniments.

It appeals to more young people than Yang-ge does due to its sophisticated movements.

Purple Bamboo Park

A Cardiovascular Workout with Fans

Yuyuantan Park

Ms. Kong is learning Mongolian chopsticks dance from Mr. Wang in *Purple Bamboo Park.*

A Lifetime Student of Play

Ms. Kong has a bagful of toys: fans, castanets, two bundles of chopsticks, handkerchiefs and so on. "I've learned more than ten different ways of playing. After I master one I move on to another and there is always stuff to learn," says Ms. Kong who has learned many forms of dance as well as Taiji sword and Taiji fan. Her fascination for park activities makes her a lifetime student of play.

7.3 Folk Dance

Dai Dance

Tibetan Dance

Mongolian Dance

Korean Dance

Residents dressed in different minority clothes to celebrate May 1st, International Labor Day in *Purple Bamboo Park*, organized by local community centers.

About the Folk Dance

According to *China Art Encyclopedia*, there are about 572 categories of dance from all 56 ethnic groups in China. Each ethnic group has unique and exquisite style of dance which makes Chinese folk-dance rich and vibrant.

In a typical park like *Purple Bamboo Park*, you may come across the Peacock dance from the *Dai* minority, the Long Sleeves dance from Tibet, and the Chopstick dance from Mongolia. The whole repertoire lasts about two hours every morning.

More than a hundred people are practicing folk dance in *Yuyuantan Park*.
One common morning scene in many parks is the aerobic-like array of people enjoying different ethnic dances.

Spin that handkerchief!
An exciting folk dance originated from Dongbei region, northeast of China

The Smile

Ms. Liu, 58, has the most precious smile in the city, irresistible, genuine, ice-melting, and contagious. She has been dancing with the morning dancing team for the last three years in *Beihai Park*.

"Dancing puts me in a good mood," she says. And her smile is the best reflection of that.

Props like rings, balls, can shakers, handkerchiefs, fans, and so on are used to keep the dance group - *Rhyme of the Ocean* - moving for about two hours each morning.

Mister Moves

"If I don't move myself, how could I move others?" says Mr. Yin, 75, dances with his emotional outpourings to interpret the music.

Whether it is a uninhibited and powerful Mongolian dance or it is a lyric fan dance, Mr. Yin gives himself 100 percent to the moment and gets a lot of more out of it. The act of self-expression is liberating; the feelings of self-fulfillment are gratifying.

This is what he enjoys and this is what he is good at - to move himself in order to move others.

Mr. Yin in *Purple Bamboo Park*

Mr. Wang (in black), who shows natural ability in Mongolian dance, attracts many followers including Mr. Yin (center).

7.4 Ballroom Dance

About Ballroom Dance in China

Ballroom dance came to China through a few major coastal cities such as Shanghai and Guangzhou, which were trading ports around the turn of the twentieth century. Public formal dancing started spreading into the inner cities after 1911.

During the early 1950s and 1960s, it was very popular in China, but was suspended during the Cultural Revolution (1966-1976). Not until the 1980s, did people feel comfortable expressing themselves in public again.

The square in *Taoranting Park* attracts hundreds of ballroom dancers on a Sunday morning with a loudspeaker keeping the beat.

Beihai Park

The sites might be casual, yet many enthusiasts take their practice seriously. Judging from the way they carry themselves, you would have no doubt that they could be in an international ballroom dance competition.

A summer night is danced away with such drama on *Beijing Exhibition Square*.

A Popular Way of Get-Moving

Among all the activities recorded in this book, ballroom dance has to be the most popular one. By Oct. 2007, the city sees at least 500 non-commercial dancing sites, according to *Beijing Daily*.

Ardent ballroom dancers can be so creative finding dance floors in parks, squares, sidewalks....

Doesn't it put a smile on your face to think that this dance form, which is conducted formally in the west, now is enjoyed by masses of Chinese in such casual manners?

A day time parking lot in front of a shopping mall turns into a perfect dance floor in the evening. These are our parents having fun with a Waltz.

"One, two, three," a ballroom-dance teacher (lady in blue skirt) and her dedicated students with imaginary partners. *Purple bamboo Park*

Learning in *Beihai Park*

No dress code required. *Yuyantan Park* (top) and Temple of *Heaven Park*.

7.5 Free Style

Mr. Zhao dances in *Purple Bamboo Park* in the morning and on the square of *Beijing Exhibition Center* at night.

Self-Made Yang-ge-Disco King

In his 50s, Mr. Zhao is quite a character. He likes to dance solo. Borrowing the music from the ballroom dance group to his right, he is having a ball himself. Rolling Yang-ge, disco and aerobic in one, his dance is indeed unique and inventive.

"Dancing gives me a great workout that keeps me healthy and happy. Only when you are healthy and happy, you can help others to be healthy and happy and only then can you enjoy your life," says Mr. Zhao as he wipes sweat from his forehead.

Shall I dance?

From the wheelchair to the dance floor, Ms. Qiu, 68, invites herself to the morning ballroom dance in *Temple of Heaven Park* everyday for the last nine years.

There is no one to please but herself. She dances to feel good and beautiful. Most of all, dancing is the sublime therapy which is really healing her - dancing is what restores her ability to walk.

In 1997, Ms. Qiu was paralyzed by a cerebral thrombosis. After she was released from the hospital, a wheelchair was waiting for her at home. But nine years later, watching her dance, one can not tell all that she has been through. Her head is up, her body moves gracefully to the music, spontaneous and whimsical, full of energy and life. The smile on her face shows that she is deeply in love with the dance she creates and the joy that comes with it. "No matter what happens in my life, being optimistic is the best medicine I can have."

7.6 Ribbon Dance

Like Yang-ge, ribbon dance is another traditional Chinese folk dance. Today it has become a popular art form used by locals for fitness-and-entertainment purpose.

Temple of Heaven Park

Beihai Park

The *Square of Beijing Exhibition Center*

Temple of Heaven Park

Let's Get Musical

A Beijing subway ticket honors the precious cultural heritage of a folk musical group formed by five different instrument players. This particular kind of music, Wuyin (five tunes) Drum is facing the danger of extinction.

8.1 Solo Singing

8.2 Chorus

8.3 Beijing Opera

8.4 Dance to the
Harmonicas

8.5 Self-organized
Performing Group

8.6 Folk Music Players

8.1 Solo Singing

Having an urge to sing?

Don't just sing in the shower because it is quite normal to sing in public in Beijing, especially in parks, solo or chorus.

Opening her heart to the lake in *Yuyuantan Park,* the lady enjoys herself by singing one song after another and moving her body gracefully just likes the willows swinging along the lake.

Yuyuantan Park

An European-style opera singer practicing in *Yuanmingyuan Park*

8.2 Chorus

A community singing group

If solo is not your thing or you want to learn some new songs from a singing group, then come to the chorus.

Yuyuantan Park

Singing is good for health.
Let's sing!

Many parks have regular singing groups.

Songs are mostly old favorites from the 50s and 60s, identified as revolutionary songs, also some romantic love songs, including a few from the Soviet Union and America.

Temple of Heaven Park

Jingshan Park

Teaching and conducting, Ms. Zhang shares her singing expertise with the crowd.
Jingshan Park

The banner says: "Teach sincerely, learn patiently, and sing happily." One of the singing groups in *Jingshan Park.*

Teacher Liu attracts about a hundred students into his singing group.

Taoranting Park

Melodies from the Pavilions

A pavilion, one of the major elements of the Chinese Garden, is not only beautiful but functional.

Folks like to get together under this architectural delight to share their common interest in singing.

Ritan Park

"Singing is a natural face-lift," the accordionist says to his choir

Sing-along session at one of the famous Five Dragon Pavilions in *Beihai Park*. At the same time, Beijing Opera singing and harmonica playing are taking place at the other two adjoining pavilions.

My favorites, though, were the singers. I have seen few things as nakedly joyful as a group of neighbors gathered in the slanting light of morning to sing their lungs out. Watching them, cynicism became impossible.

—Ben Brazil, special to The Washington Post, *"Beijing's Moment"*

8.3 Beijing Opera

About Beijing Opera

This two-century old performing art is the most popular and influential form of traditional opera in China. It is a comprehensive art form that integrates stylized acting, singing, dialogue, mime, music, dance, acrobatics, martial arts, and literature on stage to tell a story. The typical repertoire consists of ancient fairytales, legendary or classical literature from preceding dynasties.

The westerners may find the colorful facial makeup, elaborate and exquisite costumes, acrobatics and martial-art fighting on stage fascinating, but the locals are fond of the peculiar melody of Beijing Opera which captures their hearts and souls. Many of them take singing or playing the opera music as hobbies or pastimes.

Singing with a live band, this gentleman's authentic Beijing Opera attracts a big crowd in the long corridor of *Temple of Heaven Park*.

A lady is singing Ping Opera, another form of local opera, with her karaoke set in the long corridor of *Temple of Heaven Park*.

So into it, the facial expression of the Beijing Opera singer tells more about the story than his words do.

A young opera singer in *Yuyuantan Park*

Yuyuantan Park

Have the courage to sing solo in public?
Bring your own karaoke set to the park, find yourself a nice spot and you will get some audience or even some fans.

A Beijing Opera lover stages his talent show at the north gate of *Temple of Heaven Park* and attracts a young fan.

About the Instruments of Beijing Opera

Music in Beijing Opera is an ensemble of orchestral instruments and percussion. In the orchestral group, the chief instrument is "Huqin", a two-stringed bowed instrument including *Jinghu* and *Erhu* (*Jinghu* has a higher register than that of *Erhu*), and then there are *Yueqin*, a four-stringed plucked instrument with a full-moon-shaped sound box and *Sanxian*, a three-stringed plucked instrument. Suona, a high pitched horn and a flute are some of the wind instruments. The percussion group includes gongs, drums, cymbals, wooden clappers and so on which are for producing the special effects.

Impromptu neighborhood orchestra practises on an early morning

Jinghu alone can provide decent tunes for Beijing Opera.

There is a circle of Jinghu players gathering at the same spot everyday in *Temple of Heaven Park*. Some opera singers will pair up with the Jinghu players and sing some parts of a favorite repertoire.

8.4 Dance to the Harmonicas

Beijing Happy Harmonica Team in *Temple of Heaven Park*.
The team performs at the *Temple of Heaven* on Sunday mornings, *Jingshan Park* Saturdays, *Beihai Park* Thursdays and among four to five other parks randomly Tuesdays.

Harmonicas and dance, what a combination. There are several self-organized harmonica teams that perform in parks around Beijing. Some of them incorporate dancing as their total performing package to the public and some of them attract volunteer dancers from their audience. In any case, the entertainment is free.

A harmonica group playing in *Jingshan Park*

"Jingle Bells" is played by the harmonica team in an apartment compound located in southwest Beijing

A Volunteer Cheerleader

Mr. Liu, 70, has been following the *Beijing Happy Harmonic Team* for almost a year to enjoy the performance as well as to act like a cheerleader for the team. "My health gets much better by following the team from park to park. My shouting helps improve my lung capacity and blood circulation," says Mr. Liu who feels so grateful for the team and has written a poem to tell the benefit of getting out the house and engaging in healthy and happy activity like this. "Walk out the door to the musical and have a good time out while saving water, electricity, and gas at home."

"One-two," Mr. Liu, the head of the audience of the *Beijing Happy Harmonic Team*, shouts to the crowd. "Good!" the crowd shouts back, just to show their appreciation and support.

Beijing Happy Harmonic Team in *Yuyuantan Park*
and in *Temple of Heaven Park* (below)

Beijing Happy Harmonica Team in *Beihai Park*

8.5 Self-organized Performing Group

An impromptu dance from an audience member inspired by a catchy melody
from the *Xinzhu Folk Ensemble*

Mr. He is very versatile. He can conduct, play musical instruments and sing.

The ten-year-old *Xinzhu Folk Ensemble* is formed by a group of musicians who are fond of various Chinese traditional folk instruments. This musical group gives a free concert in *Yuyuantan Park* every Sunday morning and has a regular fan base of several hundred.

The *Xinzhu Folk Ensemble* has regular singers whose vocal capabilities are just as good as the professionals.

8.6 Folk Music Players

A jam session in a park
One plays the *Sheng* (left) and the other *Suona*.

Four Categories of Chinese Folk Instruments

Wind: flute, Suona, Sheng, Xiao...
Percussion: drums, gongs, cymbals, bells, metal and wooden clappers...
Plucked: Zheng, Piba, Yangqin, Yueqin, Dongbula...
Bowed: Erhu, Xanhu, Sihu, Gaohu, Jinghu, Matouqin...

吹～拉～弹～唱

A little drummer accompanied by his grandparents in *Temple of Heaven Park*. Grandpa is playing a Chinese flute.

Hulusi, made of gourd and pipes, is a famous *Dai* minority instrument which enjoys popularity in Beijing.

Melodies along the lake in Yuyuantan Park

A regular *Erhu* (a two-string bowed instrument) musician with his regular singers

"Music sounds better next to the water," says Ms. Wang, the *Guzheng* (Chinese zither) player.

An *Erhu* lesson

Social Groups

A pair of Mandarin ducks symbolizes romantic harmony.
(A glazed tile screen in Forbidden City.)

9.1 Matchmaking Meet

9.2 Emotional Support Groups

9.1 Matchmaking Meet

Outsiders are passing by and wondering what is going on.

About Matchmaking Meet

HISTORY:

Matchmaking has a long history in China. Even today many marriages are results of introductions arranged by parents. In *Changpuhe Park*, it started in 2004 when a group of middle-aged parents chatted after their morning exercise and discovered that they had one problem in common - their adult children in their late 20s or 30s still couldn't find girlfriends or boyfriends either because they were too busy or too shy or for whatever reason. After exchanging their kids' photos and helping set up their dates, some parents have made successful matches for their kids.

Over the years, it attracts thousands of people and finally the event grew into a well-known regular matchmaking meet.

Parents exchange information and photos. If they like what they see, they will swap telephone numbers and arrange blind dates for their children.

OTHER LOCATIONS:

The weekly Sunday meet in *Zhongshan Park* is probably the largest with close to 1,000 people sometimes and the one in *Yuyuantan Park* is known mostly for white collar singles.

The Matchmaking Meet in Changpuhe Park

菖蒲河公园·鹊桥会

    Every Saturday morning, in *Changpuhe Park* (located at the east side of Tian'anmen), there are about a hundred people gathering here along the long corridor, chatting and exchanging information about themselves or their adult children. This is the matchmaking meet called Magpie Bridge Meet, named after a folk story about two separated lovers brought together by a magical bridge formed by magpies.

Changpuhe Park

With this non-intimidating and pressure-free atmosphere, the park provides a pleasant venue for matchmaking meets. It doesn't matter if the result is a successful one or not; the experience raises a sense of possibility. It is also an interesting way to socialize and to make friends. Many parents who come here for their kids have given up on matchmaking agencies and other commercial enterprises.

9.2 Emotional Support Groups

爱
心
组
织

The green calligraphy carved in the rock says "Life's Oasis."

In the western corner of *Yuyuantan Park*, the big rock anchors the spot for the cancer emotional support organization called "Anti-Cancer Club". This is the place for people to find solace, hope, and courage to combat the disease and to extend their lives.

About the Emotional Support Group

Founded by a group of cancer patients in 1990, the organization, "Anti-Cancer Club" got immediate attention and support from the government. Now it is a well-established group under the Red Cross of Beijing.

It has sixteen branches scattered around different parks in Beijing such as *Beihai Park*, *Summer Palace*, and *Dragon Pool Park*. Seven of them offer year-round health therapy, comprehensive information and knowledge on combating the disease.

For more information on Beijing "Anti-Cancer Club", please visit http://bjacc.cn/htdocs1/htdocs1/English.htm.

Collective information on cancer from all sources is on display at the "Life's Oasis."

Life's Oasis

Four times a week, people with cancer may come to "Life's Oasis" in *Yuyuantan Park* to exchange experience and knowledge and to share emotional support for each other.

Every last Sunday of each month, the club offers a professional consulting session. There will be specialists in cancer therapy and drug manufacturers who can provide the latest information on treatment of the disease. Also people who recovered from cancer come to the session to share their success stories.

Cancer patients are doing *Guolin Qigong* at the "Life's Oasis."

Celebrating Life

A celebration of cancer survivors who have survived five or a multiple of five years takes place every year in September. It is called the "Five-Year-Old Birthday Party" of the cancer survivors.

Two hundred and ninety-nine people had their birthday celebrated in 2005. Among them 158 people survived 5 years, 87 people 10 years, 36 people 15 years, 10 people 20 years, 4 people 25 years, 3 people 30 years and 1 person 65 years.

On each birthday, survivor will get on the stage and be honored with a big red "Glory Flower" to wear on his or her chest, as well as some birthday presents to take home, and then they will get their group photo taken. "This is our own holiday," says one of the patients.

Of course, no celebration can be a great one without singing and dancing. The performing group formed by talented cancer patients and survivors gives a wonderful show each year during the celebration. They not only perform on their special holiday in September, but also in April of each year, when the annual "Anti-Cancer Club" celebration takes place. They also go to hospitals and prisons to perform. Their love for life has moved and encouraged many people.

Cancer survivors' birthday party in 2005. (Source: "Anti-Cancer Club" Magazine, 1st Issue 2005.)

Ms. Liou at the "Life's Oasis" in *Yuyuantan Park*

The Healing Garden

Once a bladder-cancer patient, Ms. Liou, who is from Guizhou province, comes to Beijing regularly for her annual checkup and the results have been negative for the past five years. "The garden here (Life's Oasis) is well known among cancer patients. During my medical treatment in Beijing five years ago, I came here a lot and it helped me so much. Though I'm recovered now, I still come here whenever I visit Beijing. This garden has a really good-and-positive energy field that helps people heal."

Yuyuantan Park - home to Life's Oasis

10

Special Features

10.1 The Square of the Beijing Exhibition Center
Day and Night

10.2 Other Activities

10.1 The Square of the Beijing Exhibition Center: Day and Night

Come to the Square to Feel the Vibration of Color and Sound

A Daily Gathering Place for Celebrating Life

Beijing Exhibition Center is located in the west district of Beijing. It was built in the 1950s with Russian influence. In front of it is a big square, the size of a football field and it is one of the major places for people to entertain themselves, especially during the night.

Local folks like to take advantage of this oversized, open space to do kite flying, roller skating and other activities. Since the late 1990's, ballroom dancing, Yang-ge (see Chapter 7), step dancing, as well as various dancing lessons have been taking place here during the night.

When most of the white-collar workers and other high-income people are in nightclubs, discos, theaters, fitness clubs, and so on, the rest of the folks gather on the square, having a great time for free.

It is more than celebration

It is a way of life

Happy Everyday

The *Star Light Folk Art Troupe* formed by local retirees, comes here every night for Yang-ge parade. The *Troupe* performs waist-drum on Monday mornings, daytime Yang-ge Wednesdays, and Huahui (a variety of folk-story-telling show) Fridays.

Getting ready for the parade.
Folks from the *Star Light Folk Art Troupe* are putting makeup and costumes on.
Soon you will discover that the spirit of folklore comes to life.

Let the Fun Begin

The *Troupe* enacts the story of the Monkey King, a household figure from a classical fiction "Journey to the West" which recounts the journey of the monk Xuanzang, who travels to India in search of Buddhist scriptures along with three escorts. Notice the evil witch (in the white gown) is trying to seduce the pig (in black) in an attempt to eat the monk (in the red-and-gold robe) so that she can become immortal. It is the Monkey King who sees through the plot and prevents the tragedy from happening again and again along the journey.

"Little Cart Meet", a traditional folk parade program is usually performed in the countryside.
Today it has become a vibrant city-show.
Ms. Yang (center), 54, pulls, jumps, and makes faces to excite the crowd.

Craving for Country Food

After performing this country-style entertainment, Ms. Yang is craving for some country food. She suggests to her teammates to go to a village to sample some local dishes.

Going to the outskirts of Beijing to experience the country life has become popular in recent years among urbanites. Country activities include U-pick fruits, family-style village banquets, hiking, boating, horseback riding and local folk shows.

The Chinese folklore is at its most authentic with the color, sound and people's passion, love, and fondness for a good time.

Ladies like to dress like old-fashioned housewives or matchmakers and to march to the beat of folk instruments.

A match maker who acts like a clown, a common role in folk fairs

The Night on the Square

    The square is occupied by more people during the night than that of the daytime.

    Every night, kids with parents from nearby neighborhoods, young people, retirees, and migrant workers are pouring into the square.

The *Star Light Folk Art Troupe at night*

The Drum Breaker

He thunders his raw energy out of his body and transforms it into this rhythmic-and-joyful sound that moves hundreds of Yang-ge feet on the square.

The young Yang-ge drummer is a celebrity of the square during the night. Although some of his team players have complained that they have to change the drum so often because he hits it too hard. He does attract the second largest crowd compared to the crowd of line-disco dancers.

The Drum Follower

If there is the sound of a drum, he will be there. Mr. Tian, 75, likes Yang-ge the most compared to other activities he enjoys. He has lost about 20 lbs since he started Yang-ge dancing a few years ago.

"The rhythm of drum makes me excited. I think of nothing but being happy and I realize that this is the essence of life," he says. "I feel that my spirit and energy are just as high as that of young people."

The Laughter Maker

Among the 40-to-50 Yang-ge dancers in a marching formation, there is an independent clown-dancer who does his own moves, mingling in and out of the Yang-ge parade to make people laugh and cheer.

Mr. Zheng, 65, wears a self-designed costume which looks like the costume of a clown character from the Beijing Opera. "Coming here every night makes me feel good. If I have a minor cold, after the evening dance, my sweat will fix it. I can feel that my overall health is improving and I haven't visited the hospital for the last three years since I started dancing here every night." He is so proud of his therapy for maintaining good health.

There are hundreds of spectators every night to watch the Yang-ge parade, and Mr. Zheng's appearance in the crowds always makes the night more exhilarating and interesting. "I make everybody laugh except hospitals," he must be thinking about the common saying "laughter is the best medicine," and offering his "laughing therapy" to the world around him.

Mr. Zheng is in his self-designed costume.

He is showing his signature Yang-ge move in front of the day-time folk parade.

The line-disco group (the blurred figures) draws the largest number of audience who are mostly migrant workers from the countryside.

Bravo! The Square!

Most of the onlookers on the square are migrant workers coming from all parts of China, mostly poor countryside. They are the ones who build thousands of buildings and roads in Beijing and other big cities. Yet their income is among the lowest because of the cheap man-power rate in China. Since their room and board are normally provided by their employers, they send most of their money back to their families.

The daily-evening events on the square provide these folks with free live entertainment. Some brave ones like Mr. Zhu (see his story on the next page) don't just look; they join in as well.

Hundreds of people enjoy this line-up disco every night, and most of them are young people.

Mr. Zhu is a regular spectator on the square and one day he decides to become a player himself.

From a Spectator to a Player

Mr. Zhu, 39, is a migrant worker from Henai Province, southwest of Beijing. He works as a janitor in one of the big buildings next to the square and comes here for the free entertainment every night.

To our surprise, when we last see him, he is not in the audience; instead, he becomes a Yang-ge player himself. Imitating the dancers in the parade, he is swinging silk handkerchiefs while walking to the thump of drumbeat.

From a spectator to a participant, the migrant worker is experiencing the fun side of the city life.

The daily Yang-ge parade on the square

10.2 Other Activities

1. Leg Stretching

The legs age first as we grow older.

—Chinese folk refrain

人老先老腿

Regular Leg Stretching

"A gentle, long stretch to the ligaments of legs and spine with relaxed breathing will help nourish the bones and strengthen the muscles over time," says Mr. Ma (above), 83, in *Changpuhe Park*, who feels that daily stretching has helped him alleviate pain around the knees and back. It also helps him maximize range of motion, so he can put on his socks and shoes without difficulty.

Winter morning in *Yuyuantan Park*

Omnipresent Leg Stretching
The need for stretching the legs is not exclusive to ballerinas in the training room, as you can see people like to stretch their legs in any convenient place they can find.

2. Meditating

Nature does not have attachment.
Without attachment, the heart becomes quiet;
In this manner the whole world is made tranquil.

—Laozi (Lao Tzu), *Dao De Jing (Tao Te Ching)*

A quiet connection with nature.
Two gentlemen (above and below) by the lake in *Yuyuantan Park*

Meditative Walk

"Walking is my way of meditating. It helps me balance the body and mind," says Mr. Huang who walks around the lake of *Yuyuantan Park* every morning. "I will be 89 tomorrow," he announces with pride.

Watching Mr. Huang walk with steady steps and straight body, and most important, with self-assurance about his life entering the 90s is inspiring.

The Five Dragon Pavilions in *Beihai Park*

Parks and Park-Goers

When the pagoda standing on the hill glows to the sunrise,
The lake smiles.

When the breeze teaches the weeping willow how to dance,
The pavilion envies.

When the white marble bridge arches its back to tiptoe across
the water,
The lotus blushes.

When the bird sings the first morning song,
Beijing resonates.

When the morning park-goers resume their spots,
The park conspires to play.

(Dongmei Lu)

BEIJING AT A GLANCE

POPULATION

Beijing had a registered population of 15.81 million in 2006.

The average life span of Beijingers was 79.80 years in 2005. The average life expectancy of Beijingers is expected to reach 80 by 2010 as the health of local people is improving steadily, according to local health authorities.

PEOPLE

There are 56 ethnic groups in China. The majority of the population is the Han ethnic group, making up 90 percent of the total population. People of all 56 ethnic groups are found in Beijing.

THE CAPITAL

Beijing was the capital of five dynasties: Liao (907-1125), Jin (1115-1234), Yuan (1206-1368), Ming (1368-1644), and Qing (1644-1911) dynasties. Since October 1st, 1949, Beijing has been the capital of the People's Republic China.

CLIMATE

Categorized as a "continental monsoon" climate, Beijing belongs to the warm temperate zone with semi-humid climate. It has four distinctive seasons with short springs and falls while summers and winters are long. January is the coldest month with temperatures as low as 10 °F and July is the hottest month with temperatures as high as 100 °F.

PARKS IN BEIJING

IMPERIAL GARDENS

For more than 800 years, emperors of past dynasties had ordered the construction of palaces, gardens, temples, and retreats for imperial use. Some of the major imperial parks are *Beihai*, *Jingshan*, *Summer Palace, Temple of Heaven*, and *Fragrant Hills*. Today these places have been retained and restored for the enjoyment of the general public.

PUBLIC PARKS

Besides the parks built in previous dynasties, there are over one hundred parks that have been built since to accommodate the growing population. As of June 2006, there are 169 registered parks in Beijing and 123 of them are free of admission. An annual pass, which is good for 17 popular parks in Beijing, can be purchased at a great price around the beginning of each year. Also each park offers a monthly pass to the public at a discounted price.

The total number of annual passes sold in 2006 was 1.251 million increasing to 1.558 million in 2007 according to the Beijing Municipal Administration Center of Parks.

FUNCTIONS AND TRENDS

Secluded among the hustle and bustle of the big city, Beijing parks provide beautiful and calm environments for people to rest, relax, exercise, entertain, and socialize. In recent years, more and more public parks have become lifestyle centers.

Fragrant Hills
香山公园

Summer Palace
颐和园

Yuanmingyuan
圆明园

★ Purple Bamboo Park
紫竹院公园

Beijing Exhibit
Center
北京展览馆

Linglong Park
玲珑公园

★ Yuyuantan Park
玉渊潭公园

Map of the Major Parks in Beijing

Relative locations of some of the parks and landmarks
mentioned in this book (not to scale).

★ Recommended for observing park activities

4th Ring Road

N
S

Yuandadu Park
元大都遗址公园

3rd Ring Road

Temple of Earth Park
地坛公园

2nd Ring Road

Drum & Bell
钟鼓楼

2nd North Ring
Sidewalk Park
北二环公园

Shichahai Lake
什刹海

Beihai Park
北海公园

Jingshan Park
景山公园

Forbidden City
故宫

Chaoyang Park
朝阳公园

Changpuhe Park
菖蒲河公园

Ritan Park
日坛公园

Tuanjiehu Park
团结湖公园

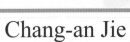

Chang-an Jie

Tian'anmen
天安门

Dongdan Park
东单公园

Qianmen
前门

Taoranting Park
陶然亭公园

Temple of Heaven
天坛

Dragon Pool Park
龙潭公园

How We Did It

I (Hongmei) initiated the idea for this book at the end of 2005. My sister Dongmei responded enthusiastically. We both thought it was something interesting and meaningful and decided to do the project together.

Dongmei by the *Shichahai Lake*

The first trip from San Francisco to Beijing was made in Feb 21st, 2006 to catch winter season and, as a bonus, to enjoy the Spring Festival (Chinese New Year) with our parents who live there. The experience was fantastic! And luckily we caught beautiful snow scenes of Beijing.

Hongmei by the *Shichahai Lake*

From then on, each of us made two more trips, one of which overlapped so we had chance to work together. By the end of 2006, we had covered winter, spring, summer, and autumn while gathering over 5,000 photos and hours of video.

The second half of the project was the book writing and designing aided by publishing software. We have to say, it was not as fun as doing the research in Beijing parks, shooting photos and interviewing people.

Hongmei interviews Mr. Fang, 89, who walks every morning in *Yuyuantan Park*.

Hours and hours of sitting in front of computers, countless arguments over which photos were to be used (It wasn't easy to give up so many photos, especially those to which we had personal attachment), what size they should be, how to express an idea more effectively, and many other issues. Nonetheless, the good news is we always come to agreement in the end.

Barbara Manfredi, Dongmei's friend and editorial reader

By the end of 2007, the book is finally completed! Neither of us has done anything like this before, but thanks to the modern technology, the convenience of Internet for gathering information, and software on book making and designing, we were able to do it. Naturally, we could not do a project whose focus is half way around the world, without the support and input from our husbands, parents and friends. Most important, we would not have been able to do it without the friendliness and openness of the Beijing park-goers.

AFTERWORD

We wanted to make a record of the proliferating activities that captured our hearts when we visited the parks in Beijing – activities that reveal the spirit of the Chinese people at this particular time in history; activities that have been inherited from history; activities that have been reinvented since the end of the Cultural Revolution in 1976; activities that seem common and negligible to the locals who live in the midst of the park culture; moreover, activities, like some of the wonders of old Beijing, that might disappear when the next generation of Beijingers comes into play.

(Please note that new activities continue to evolve as this book goes to press and the park culture is not limited to Beijing - city after city throughout China enjoy similar activities powered by the same playful spirit.)

As the work progressed, we felt more and more excited about this project. Every trip we made to the parks in Beijing has enriched us in some way and there was always something unexpected around the corner. Many new friends were made along the way and many stories were discovered. Uplifting and inspiring, it truly has been a great experience for us. As a result of making this book, our attitudes towards life and health have been changed – we have become more positive and active. Hongmei, encouraged by the winter swimmers has picked up swimming as a daily activity and Dongmei has made up her mind – to be ever playful.

We hope that this book will be inspirational to you as well as entertaining.

Wishing you a healthy and happy life!

Hongmei Lu & Dongmei Lu

Acknowledgements

To our parents, Zhongshi Lu and Lanying Zhou for their encouragement and trust in us;

To our husbands, Robert Hallewell and Michael Scoggins for all their support;

To our editorial reader Barbara Manfredi for her kind assistance in English;

To our friends Wei Manfredi, Debi Maesaka, Qi Lin, Karen Hansen, Jeff Hansen, Erin Scoggins, and Zengyu Cheng for their emotional support and many valuable suggestions;

To Paul Manfredi, assistant professor of Chinese, and Chair, Chinese Studies at Pacific Lutheran University, who helped us with the introduction.

Finally, we feel real fortunate to work with our editor Meijing Zhang, our art editor Zhijie Yan, and art designer Peng Liu who did such a wonderful and efficient job.

About the Authors

Hongmei is an artist and holds a MFA from the Academy of Art University, San Francisco.

Dongmei holds a BS in Electrical Engineering from the University of California at Davis and worked as a design engineer at Intel Corporation.

Hongmei Lu and Dongmei Lu were born and raised in Beijing and have been lived on the west coast of the United States for more than ten years.

Bibliography

Books in Chinese

Zhi, Tu. *Huangdi Neijing: Understanding the Chinese Style Health Care*. Xi'an, Shaanxi: Shaanxi Normal University Press, 2006.

Sun, Jianhua. *Exploring Beijing*. Beijing: China Social Sciences Press, 2004.

Li, Lulu. *An Illustration to the Chinese Traditional Toys and Games*. Xi'an, Shaanxi: World Publishing Corporation, 2005.

Books in English

Lin, Yutang. *My Country and My People*. New York: The John Day Company, 1939.

Brahm, Laurence. *Elements of China: WATER WOOD FIRE EARTH GOLD*
Beijing: China Intercontinental Press, 2002.

Buchanan, Keith. China: *The Land and the People*. New York: Crown Publishers, Inc., 1980.

Morrison, Hedda. *A Photographer in Old Peking*. New York: Oxford University Press, 1985.

Master Liang, Shou-Yu & Wu, Wen-Ching. *Tai Chi Chuan: 24 & 48 Posture with Martial Applications*. Roslindale, MA: YMAA Publication Center, 1996.

Kuo, Simmone. *Long Life Good Health trough Tai-Chi Chuan*. Berkeley, CA: North Atlantic Books, 1991.

Jahnke, Roger. *The Healing Promise of Qi: Creating Extraordinary Wellness Through Qigong and Tai Chi*. New York: Contemporary Book, 2002.

McClellan, Sam. *Integrative Acupressure*. New York: The Berkley Publishing Group, 1998.

Beinfield, Harriet and Korngold, Efrem. *Between Heaven and Earth*. New York: The Ballantine Publishing Group, 1991.

Elias, Jason and Ketcham, Katherine. *Chinese Medicine for Maximum Immunity: Understanding the Five Elemental Types for Health and Well-Being*. New York: Three Rivers Press, 1999.

Dong, Paul and Esser, Aristide H. Chi Gong: *The Ancient Chinese Way to Health*. New York: Paragon House, 1990.

Dyer, Wayne. *Change Your Thoughts - Change Your Life: Living the Wisdom of the Tao*. Carlsbad, CA: Hay House, 2007.

Riseman, Tom. *Understanding the I Ching*. Hammersmith, London: Thorsons, 1995.

Veith, Ilza. *The Yellow Emperor's Classic of Internal Medicine*. Berkeley, CA: University of California Press, 1972.